EDGE BOOKS™

Video Games vs. Reality

BATTLE ZONE

THE INSPIRING **TRUTH** BEHIND POPULAR COMBAT VIDEO GAMES

BY: THOMAS KINGSLEY TROUPE

CAPSTONE PRESS
a capstone imprint

T0050827

Edge Books are published by Capstone Press,
1710 Roe Crest Drive, North Mankato, Minnesota 56003
www.mycapstone.com

Library of Congress Cataloging-in-Publication Data
Names: Troupe, Thomas Kingsley, author.
Title: Battle zone : the inspiring truth behind popular combat video games /
    by Thomas Kingsley Troupe.
Description: North Mankato, Minnesota : Capstone Press, 2019. | Series:
    Edge books. Video games vs. reality | Audience: Age 8–14.
Identifiers: LCCN 2018006071 (print) | LCCN 2018006708 (ebook) |
    ISBN 9781543525786 (eBook PDF) | ISBN 9781543525700 (hardcover) |
    ISBN 9781543525748 (paperback)
Subjects: LCSH: Military art and science--Juvenile literature. | Combat—
    Juvenile literature. | Military art and science—Computer games—Juvenile
    literature. | Combat—Computer games—Juvenile literature.
Classification: LCC U106 (ebook) | LCC U106 .T76 2019 (print) |
    DDC 793.9/20285—dc23
LC record available at https://lccn.loc.gov/2018006071

Editorial Credits
Aaron Sautter, editor; Kyle Grenz, designer; Tracy Cummins, media researcher;
    Tori Abraham, production specialist

Photo Credits
Alamy: vanillasky, 24 Top; EA: Battlefield: Bad Company 2 Vietnam image used
with permission of Electronic Arts Inc., 19, Medal of Honor: Rising Sun image
used with permission of Electronic Arts Inc., 13 Bottom; Flickr: www.army.
mil/Air Force photo by Staff Sgt. Jason T. Bailey, 26; Getty Images: Bloomberg/
Troy Harvey, 27, Chesnot, 11, 17, Hulton Archive, 8–9, 18, IWM/Sgt. D M
Smith, 15, Sovfoto, 20, Terry Fincher, 22; iStockphoto: LifeJourneys, 6–7 Top;
Library of Congress: 25; NARA: WAR & CONFLICT BOOK, 12; Shutterstock:
breakermaximus, 4–5, CreativeCore, Design Element, enjoy your life, Design
Element, Everett Historical, 10, 13 Top, 14, 28–29, Lukasz Szwaj, Design Element,
Maxim Apryatin, Cover Middle, Podsolnukh, Design Element, Roka Pics, 7,
Serhiy Smirnov, Design Element; Wikimedia: 21, www.defenseimagery.mil, 16

Printed and bound in the United States of America.
PA017

TABLE OF CONTENTS

CHAPTER 1

On Your Feet, Soldier!

A mortar shell slams into the ground a few yards away. The ground shakes. Your ears ring as clumps of dirt rain down around you. Your squad mate reloads his weapon and nods to you. You adjust your helmet and check your ammo. It's now or never. Your team has suffered heavy losses, but you need to retake the hill and drive the enemy back. You signal to your partner. He pops up from your **foxhole**, firing his rifle at the enemy's position.

foxhole—a small pit, usually for one or two soldiers, dug as a shelter in a battle area

When you scramble out of the hole, enemy forces start firing. Bullets strike the muddy earth at your boots. There's a loud *ting* as a bullet glances off of your helmet.

Across the battlefield, you see some large military crates stacked near a shed. You rip a grenade from your belt and pull the pin. The enemy is shouting and firing as you lob the explosive toward the crates. They dive for cover just as their hidden ammo dump explodes. The blast lights up the sky over the smoky battle zone.

During World War II (1939–1945) brave soldiers faced many dangers on the battlefield. These included enemy gunfire, grenades, powerful military vehicles, and many more.

Congratulations! You've survived the battle. But this wasn't real-life combat. It was all a game, taking place within a **virtual** world. Military forces and historical wars have long inspired video games. Combat games are incredibly popular. In fact, they have been some of the best-selling game titles of all time. Stepping into the boots of a battle-hardened soldier can really get the blood racing.

virtual—not real; when something is made to seem real on a computer

Game designers know that players enjoy the rush of fighting in simulated combat. They study military history to bring the feel of real combat into their games. They research military gear, weapons, and vehicles. Game designers recreate history's greatest battles for players to experience for themselves.

simulated—when something is made to look and feel like the real thing

CHAPTER 2

Wars of the World

Many military-based games use an actual war as a starting point. Most combat games are first-person shooters that show battles through a soldier's eyes. With careful attention to detail, the locations can look almost like the real thing.

World War, Won?

It's often called The Great War or The War to End All Wars. But only a few games are set during World War I (1914–1918). The war pitted the **Allied powers** against the **Central powers**. World War I was the first time a war was fought on land, at sea, below sea, and in the skies. Unfortunately, the war was at a standstill for a long time. Both sides fought fiercely but rarely gained much ground.

Trench warfare was common during World War I. Trenches protected soldiers from enemy fire, but they were usually cold and muddy. Charging the enemy from a trench was called "going over the top."

In the game *Verdun* players get to see what combat was like during The Great War. They have to fight through fields of barbed wire fencing and muddy trenches. They must avoid enemy machine guns and poison gas. The game designers also tried to capture the back and forth feel of combat in the war. Gamers fight with a squad to capture an area and must defend it against the enemy. If the squad loses, players are returned to the starting point and have to start over again. The two sides fight back and forth until the enemy's headquarters is captured.

FACT

Over 8 million soldiers were killed during World War I, and at least 21 million were injured.

Allied powers—a group of countries that fought the Central powers in World War I; the Allies included the United States, England, France, Russia, and Italy

Central powers—a group of countries that fought the Allied powers in World War I; the Central powers included Germany, Turkey, and Austria-Hungary

World War, Too

The most popular war in combat games is World War II (1939–1945). Dozens of titles thrust players into the frontlines of history's biggest war. Possibly the biggest and most famous battle of the war was the Battle of Normandy in northern France. Known as D-Day, the invasion was launched on June 6, 1944. The goal was to establish a foothold in Europe so Allied forces could begin pushing Nazi forces back to Germany. More than 4,000 real-life Allied troops gave their lives that day.

Axis & Allies

As war raged across much of Europe and the world, the two opposing sides became known as the Axis and the Allies. In the strategy-based video game *Axis & Allies*, players assume the role of a World War II military general. A player controls when and where his or her military forces will attack. Success or failure is determined by random dice rolls by the computer.

In *Call of Duty: WWII*, players and their squad arrive on the Normandy beaches on D-Day. Their mission is to take control of the area. They need to move up the hill to take out Germany's defensive positions. The game puts players in the middle of the chaotic and deadly battle. Thankfully, no game can ever completely recreate the horrors of the Battle of Normandy. But game developers worked to make *Call of Duty: WWII* as realistic as possible. Explosions rock the beach, bullets whiz through the air, and fellow soldiers drop all around players as they advance on the beach.

No Safe Harbor

Not all battles are fought on land. On December 7, 1941, hundreds of Japanese fighter planes attacked Pearl Harbor near Honolulu, Hawaii. The attack on the U.S. Naval base caught the U.S. Navy completely off guard.

The bombing was devastating. The Japanese planes destroyed or damaged nearly 20 naval ships, including eight battleships. They also destroyed more than 300 airplanes. Nearly 2,500 Americans were killed in the attack, and 1,000 people were wounded. President Franklin D. Roosevelt declared war on Japan the next day, and the United States officially entered World War II.

In EA Games' *Medal of Honor: Rising Sun*, gamers play as Corporal Joe Griffin as he fights against Japanese forces at Pearl Harbor.

Game players can take part in the attack on Pearl Harbor in *Medal of Honor: Rising Sun*. Game designers made the game as realistic as possible. It follows the timeline of the real battle. Players are shaken from their bunks in the early morning as the first Japanese bombs hit. Players then struggle to the ship's deck to find swarms of enemy planes dropping bombs. Gamers try to fight off the planes while the ship is torn up all around them.

FACT

The USS *Arizona*, a battleship sunk during the attack on Pearl Harbor, was turned into a memorial. The site draws more than 1.8 million visitors from around the world each year.

Medal of Honor: Rising Sun used with permission of Electronic Arts Inc.

CHAPTER 3

Overwhelming Odds

Game designers often test players by sending wave after wave of enemies at them. This gives gamers a feel for the danger soldiers faced on the battlefield. As in real combat, the odds of survival may not be in the player's favor.

Not a Lovely Garden

Operation Market Garden during World War II was known as history's greatest **airborne** assault. The plan was to surround and take over a German stronghold in the Netherlands. Allied **paratroopers** would land behind enemy lines and take control of the bridges.

airborne—military forces carried in airplanes

paratrooper—a soldier trained to jump by parachute into battle

Meanwhile, ground forces would move deeper into enemy territory. Ground troops would travel along Highway 69, securing towns along the way. Due to the deadly battles that took place during the mission, the road came to be known as Hell's Highway.

FACT

Operation Market Garden took place September 17–25, 1944. It consisted of two battle plans. Operation Market was the name for the airborne troops' plans to seize bridges. Operation Garden was the plan for Allied ground forces to push north into enemy territory.

In the game *Brothers in Arms: Hell's Highway,* players take part in Operation Market Garden. But just as the real soldiers discovered, players learn that Hitler's top soldiers and tank divisions have already dug in. The German forces fiercely defend the area. Unlike many World War II games, this one doesn't necessarily have a happy ending. The Nazis usually crush the Allied troops, just as they did during the real mission.

◄ After landing, paratroopers worked to secure key locations within dangerous enemy territory.

Operation Missed

The Battle of the Bulge, or "Operation Mist," was
Germany's last major attack in World War II. The battle
took place in eastern Belgium. On December 16, 1944,
the Germans sent 250,000 soldiers into combat, along
with five panzer tank divisions. The weather was foggy
that day. The Germans snuck in and took the Allied
forces by surprise. The Americans had only about
80,000 troops when Germany attacked.

In *Call of Duty: WWII* game designers accurately recreated the deadly setting of the Battle of the Bulge. Players can feel the desperation of U.S. forces as bullets whiz by their heads in the heavy mist. Explosions rock the countryside and knock down trees. Players fight against overwhelming enemy forces just to live and fight another day.

FACT

The U.S. forces suffered about 75,000 casualties at the Battle of the Bulge. It was one of the bloodiest battles fought by the United States in the entire war.

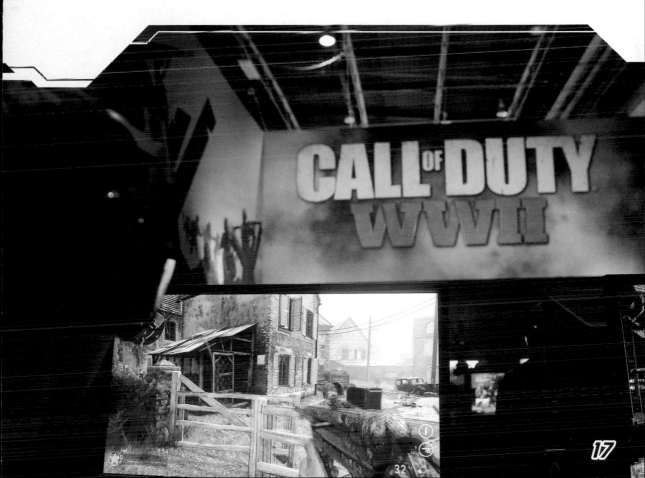

North vs. South

A few games focus on wars other than World War II. The Vietnam War (1954–1975) gives game makers a chance to drop players into a different kind of battlefield.

The Vietnam War was a conflict between North and South Vietnam. The South was a **democratic** country supported by the United States. The North, supported by the Soviet Union, wanted to rule Vietnam as a **communist** country. It was a very long and difficult conflict. Soldiers spent years fighting hidden enemies in Vietnam's jungles and swamps. In the end, the United States had to leave South Vietnam. The North took control of the entire country.

FACT

The average age of a combat soldier in the Vietnam War was 22 years old.

democratic—having a government in which citizens vote for their leaders

communist—having a system in which all the land, houses, and factories belong to the government or community

Battlefield: Bad Company 2 Vietnam puts players in combat in the thick jungles of Vietnam. Gamers can play as either American or North Vietnamese soldiers. Players who fight for the United States can use military vehicles such as tanks, helicopters, and bomber planes. Meanwhile, North Vietnamese players often use stealth tactics. They fight with anti-tank and anti-aircraft weapons. Game designers made sure both sides were balanced to reflect how difficult real combat was during the Vietnam War.

Jungle Road

The Ho Chi Minh Trail was a series of roads and paths leading from North Vietnam to South Vietnam. The North used the trail to transport troops and weapons into the South. The United States often bombed the trail to try to stop the enemy from resupplying the front lines. Over time the Ho Chi Minh Trail gained another name: "The Blood Road."

CHAPTER 4

Metal Movers

Many gamers love the thrill of battling
the enemy with a rifle and their wits. But
sometimes soldiers need greater firepower
on the frontlines. As in real-life combat,
players often rely on military vehicles to
gain an edge in battle.

◄ The Russian T-34/76 tank was equipped with a
76.2 mm (3-inch) cannon that could penetrate
armor up to 92 mm (3.6 inches) thick.

Tanks for the Assist!

Nothing strikes fear into the hearts of troops like an armored tank. The first tanks used on a battlefield were Britain's Mark I tanks at the Battle of the Somme in France on September 15, 1916. The tanks were slow and many broke down. However, they forever changed how battles are fought during wartime. Over time, tanks became stronger, faster, and delivered deadlier blasts from their turrets.

In *Call of Duty: World at War* players get the chance to control the Russian OT-34/85 Tank. But unlike real Russian tanks, the video game version is easier to defeat on the battlefield. A few well-placed grenades can stop the tank dead in its tracks. Game makers program the tanks this way to bring balance to the game. After all, it's no fun if a player is totally unstoppable.

FACT

The first British tank prototype was named Little Willie. It weighed 14 tons (12.7 metric tons) and was extremely slow. But it helped show that it was possible to safely plow through enemy lines during a gun battle.

turret—a rotating, armored structure that holds
a large weapon on top of a military vehicle

Get to the Chopper!

Having tanks on the ground is great, but sometimes you need air support. During the Vietnam War, helicopters were very important for the war effort. They were used to attack enemy targets and to carry soldiers to and from the battlefield.

The Bell UH-1 "Huey" Helicopter was one of the most widely used helicopters in the war. There were several models. Some were used for attacking enemy ground forces. They were equipped with machine guns, grenade launchers, and anti-tank missiles. Other Huey helicopters were used mainly as troop carriers. These choppers were still deadly, however. They carried machine guns to provide cover fire as soldiers got on or off the chopper.

FACT

The Huey helicopter got its nickname from its early HU-1 label. People started calling it "Huey." The helicopter's name was later switched to UH-1, but the nickname stuck.

Battlefield: Bad Company 2 Vietnam puts players into the pilot seat, allowing them to guide a Huey helicopter across Vietnam's landscape. Gamers can feel the excitement of taking out enemy camps and ground forces. They can land in hot zones to rescue soldiers during heavy combat. As an added touch, the helicopter's radio even plays rock music from that time period.

CHAPTER 5

Hand-Held Havoc

A good rifle or handgun is a soldier's best friend. Countless firearms have been used to wage war over the years. And no combat game would be complete without a variety of weapons for players to use. Game developers do their best to help players experience some of history's most iconic weapons.

Soldiers in World War II relied heavily on the M1-Garand rifle. The gun was often used as a substitute for heavier machine guns.

◄ The Call of Duty series has always provided gamers with many different weapons to fight with. These include rifles, machine guns, shotguns, grenade launchers, and many more.

A Call to Firearms

Possibly the most valued weapon of World War II was the M1-Garand. This semi-automatic rifle was light weight and could fire several shots very quickly. The M1 was great for both short- and long-range attacks. Soldiers could hit targets up to 500 yards (460 meters) away.

The M1-Garand is faithfully recreated in *Call of Duty: WWII.* It's designed to look, sound, and even act like the real thing. Just like the actual rifles, the game version has some kick to it. When fired, the weapon gets knocked off its target. Players are forced to realign the rifle after each shot. Also like the real gun, the M1 can be equipped with a scope to help with aiming at long-range targets.

FACT

One of the most realistic details of the M1-Garand in the game is the "ping" sound made when it's out of **ammunition**. It was a true-life sound that told soldier it was time to reload their rifles—and fast!

ammunition—bullets and other objects that can be fired from weapons

Boom Time

Rifles and handguns are useful in combat. But sometimes you need more powerful weapons. Missile launchers and flamethrowers cause plenty of destruction. However, a grenade launcher is often the best option on the battlefield. One of the most popular launchers used by the military is the M203. Soldiers carry them into battle and fire grenades at enemy positions from a safe distance.

Wild Weapons

Not all weapons in video games are realistic. In *Wolfenstein* a player can use a weapon known as the "Particle Cannon." It shoots a long beam of electricity that electrocutes enemies by the dozen. In the Fallout series, players can use the "Fat Man." This incredible gun can launch mini-sized nuclear bombs to destroy monsters and other enemies. Of course, even mini-sized mushroom clouds would spell big trouble for people in the real world.

In some games, such as *Ghost Recon: Wildlands*, players can modify their weapons. During the game, players may stumble across an M203 grenade launcher. Just like the real-life version, the launcher adds a second trigger to the weapon. When fired, it makes a signature *WHUMP* sound. Anything the grenade hits explodes into flaming rubble. Meanwhile, the player can stand back and safely watch the action.

FACT

The U.S. military has used the M203 grenade launcher since it replaced the M79 during the Vietnam War.

Time to Deploy!

Real-life wars and soldiers have inspired some of the most popular video games ever made. Military history provides game designers with everything they need to create amazing, action-packed video games.

The battles in combat-based games don't always happen as they did in real life. Game makers add elements of suspense and danger to keep gamers on their toes. But game designers often include accurate weapons, battles, and vehicles from the past. This added realism makes the gaming experience more fun and memorable for players.

Becoming a virtual soldier on the battlefield is a thrilling experience. Accomplishing a difficult mission gives players a sense of pride. Game companies want players to feel like they're part of the biggest battles in history. Then players will keep coming back for more.

GLOSSARY

airborne (AIR-bohrn)—military forces carried in airplanes

Allied powers (AL-lyd PAU-uhrs)—a group of countries that fought the Central powers in World War I; the Allies included the United States, England, France, Russia, and Italy

Allies (AL-lyz)—a group of countries that fought together in World War II, including France, the United States, Canada, Great Britain, the Soviet Union, and others

ammunition (am-yuh-NI-shuhn)—bullets and other objects that can be fired from weapons

Axis (AX-uhs)—a group of countries that fought together in World War II, including Germany, Italy, and Japan

Central powers (SEN-truhl PAU-uhrs)—a group of countries that fought the Allied powers in World War I; the Central powers included Germany, Turkey, and Austria-Hungary

communist (KAHM-yuh-nist)—having a system in which all the land, houses, and factories belong to the government or community

democratic (de-muh-KRAT-ik)—having a government in which citizens vote for their leaders

foxhole (FOKS-hohl)—a small pit, usually for one or two soldiers, dug as a shelter in a battle area

paratrooper (PAIR-uh-troop-ur)—a soldier trained to jump by parachute into battle

simulated (SIM-yuh-lay-tuhd)—when something is made to look and feel like the real thing

turret (TUR-it)—a rotating, armored structure that holds a large weapon on top of a military vehicle

virtual (VIR-choo-uhl)—not real; when something is made to seem real on a computer

READ MORE

Cooke, Tim. *World War II on the Front Lines.* Life on the Front Lines. North Mankato, Minn.: Capstone Press, 2015.

Micklos Jr., John. *Harlem Hellfighters: African American Heroes of World War I.* Military Heroes. North Mankato, Minn.: Capstone Press, 2017.

Williams, Brian. *World War II: Visual Encyclopedia.* New York: DK Publishing, 2015.

INTERNET SITES

Use FactHound to find Internet sites related to this book.

Visit *www.facthound.com*

Just type in 9781543525700 and go.

 Check out projects, games and lots more at **www.capstonekids.com**

INDEX